The Poetry of Farming

Also by Geoffrey Lilburne and published by Ginninderra Press
The Life Between

Geoffrey Lilburne

The Poetry of Farming

The Poetry of Farming
ISBN 978 1 76109 650 1
Copyright © text Geoffrey Lilburne 2023

First published 2023 by
GINNINDERRA PRESS
PO Box 3461 Port Adelaide 5015
www.ginninderrapress.com.au

Contents

Introduction	7
Memoir	9
Meditation on Arrival at Farm	19

The Farm Year

Early Autumn Days	23
The Coming of the Rain	24
Ploughing	25
Lap of Luxury	26
September Song	28
November Storm	29
After Harvest	30
Resting Cows	31

On Farming

Half Farmer Half Poet	35
Farming with Trees	36
Saving the Universe	37
Salt Burn	38
Morality Play	39
Bruce Rock Dreaming	40
More Land	41
Sufficiency	42

From the Hilltop

Hymn	45
After the Fire	47
The Magic Windmill	48
This my real	50
Marginal Farm	51
Gold mine	52
Seeking	53

Bountiful Acres	54
More Like a Sabbath	55

Introduction

In 1989, two events occurred which changed the course of my life. First, I purchased a small hillside farm in the beautiful Chittering Valley one hour north of the city. Next, I opened a banking account called 'Lilburne Pastoral Enterprizes' into which I deposited surplus income from such pastoral duties as funerals and weddings and out of which I paid for my first herd of rough north-west steers. The pastor was set to become a pastoralist!

In this book, I detail my growing relationship with the farm, moving from the excitement of purchase and early dreams towards something deeper and more realistic. The book is not only about fulfilling a youthful dream in middle age but also a spiritual journey of self-discovery through developing an intimate and reciprocal relationship with a plot of land. My journey has taught me something of what Indigenous brothers and sisters mean by 'country' – that is, a physical and spiritual bond which nurtures the humans as much as they might care for the land. It is the story of how a 'sense of place' transformed me.

Memoir

When you buy a farm, you are full of hopes and dreams, possibly with visions of a life on the land. Some of those hopes are fanciful and some are grounded in reality. Time alone will tell. To what extent are they rooted in who we are and the unfolding of our mortal lives?

My first vocational wish and dream was to be a farmer. As a thirteen-year-old, I could see myself working alongside my dad on our farm. His response was abrupt! 'Don't be ridiculous!' Bluntly he killed an immediate and concrete wish, but the dream lived on.

In the meantime, I resolved to train for the ministry with the aim of becoming a theologian. I published my first book in 1989 on the theology of the land. Its title was *A Sense of Place* and it forms the theological ground of what is written here. It wasn't until my forty-sixth year that I was able to buy my first farm.

Thirty years and a couple of careers had passed so that I had scraped together enough savings to invest in a parcel of land, fifty-five acres in the Chittering Valley. After such a long gestation, what shape would my farming aspirations take?

I could never be a real farmer, living off the land as I once might have wished. But how close could I come? I wasn't content to be a hobby farmer, which sounded too frivolous, self-indulgent to me. I wanted to be serious about this enterprise. Perhaps I could make some money, run some stock. Broad-acre farmer I would never be, but what about a small farmer? Well, I would jolly well give it a try.

> It's dusty gritty, dirt smudges
> every corner. No city spotless,
> rainwashed streets, ornamental trees,
> but marri, wandoo. Here
> I stake my claim as near as
> I can get to real farm.
>
> from 'This my real'

Dad was now seventy-four, but an active and energetic old man and his enthusiasm for the farm surprisingly matched my own! He had always loved projects, had built his life around them, practical projects involving work with his hands. Now the farm became our project. My adolescent dream came to fulfilment some three decades after its inception! There was very little money, so we scrounged lumber, sheet iron, tools and put up our small shed, lovingly constructed. Our first project, then came fencing, water pumping with an inefficient jet pump, then another, steel-framed, bigger shed.

Our first fencing was strained using the red Brumby ute I had acquired. The sale of the first group of red nor-wester steers brought a modest return, as did my sales of cut wandoo logs for firewood in Floreat Park homes. I tried to get Dad to organise a windmill to water our stock in summer. All he would say was, 'Wouldn't it be lovely!' He could not bring himself to make phone calls to make it happen. Maybe he was already living in the future of the farm when he was no longer there, for he said to me once or twice, 'Wouldn't it be great to have $100,000 dollars to spend on this place?' Was he, I wondered, already spending the inheritance I would, one day, receive? At a certain point, when he felt he could no longer work after a heart attack and bypass surgery, Dad gave up and came no more to the farm.

It wasn't just Dad and me. My wife Peta, a designer and landscape architect, was working hard on the design of the house we would build – again on a tight budget – on the high hillside of the property. Site works began in 1994 and the house was completed in 1995 so that we were able at the end of that year to take our summer vacation there. Now my visits to the farm could be more extended with overnight stays and long days of work.

Of course, I continued to visit weekly and discovered it to be a welcome place of quietness and solitude after a busy week in parish ministry. Soon I acquired a small disc plough and was able to plough the roadside paddock, away from the hills, and put in an oat crop, later cutting hay from it. It was now possible to plan for longer overnight stays, sometimes with Peta, sometimes alone. Those solitary times opened up for me another side of the place, as I was able to transmute my thoughts and reflections into prayer. For a while, I dreamt of making the place into a retreat centre, with some more building and planning. But my heart wasn't really in this plan and nothing came of it.

Meanwhile, the business model changed. With the completion of some fencing, I was able to grow a good little hay crop and take off a good supply of summer feed for my herd. I began buying young store steers to sell after twelve months or so. But the market vulnerability of that model soon soured on me and I bought instead a few cows and a bull from which I had a sure supply of young cattle to sell. From a business perspective, it was a much better proposition as I soon collected top dollar for my little vealers. My real farm was evolving.

The disastrous Sydney years, 1998–2006, followed, when I relocated to take up a top executive position with the national council of the Uniting Church. The move destroyed my first marriage and left me severely shaken about my future direction. I put the property in the hands of rental agents and slowly paid off more of my mortgage.

Shortly after the move, Dad died and it seemed from that point that my life fell apart. Upsetting as the loss of a much-loved parent is, it seemed odd to me that everything suddenly went wrong. Reflecting now, I can see that my separation from the farm cut me off from a spiritual resource that was truly sustaining for my life and work. At the time, I gave it no thought! It was after a hot day which suddenly gave way to rain that I smelled the fragrance of the earth and knew I needed to return to the farm.

Returning to Perth in 2006, without a job, without a wife, I resolved to take up residence at the farm. Having lived there briefly in 2004 during a long-service leave, I knew it was possible. Cash was tight and appeals to the Church office were responded to grudgingly. I was actively looking for work, and soon found a temporary placement at one of Perth's suburban churches. The hour's commute from the farm to the city was not onerous, and it worked for the time being.

Back on the farm, I resolved after my long absence to make it productive again. My little Fergy had given up the ghost, so an engine rebuild was necessary. Stock were purchased and soon I was in a position to resume my old farming model. But money was short, and my part-time city-based city work multiplied to the point where it was necessary to take up at least part-time city residence. The bond with the farm continued to be important for me, so a pattern of off-farm work and residence combined with quiet weekends with the cattle proved to be a viable combination.

I was able to spend a few months visiting Mum in her care

facilities, but our contact was largely non-verbal as she had succumbed to a form of dementia. Her death later that year meant that I had lost any parental support, but in death they were able to further my farming dreams. My inheritance enabled me to pay off debts and to spend some real money on the place, as Dad had fondly imagined. I bought a new four-wheel drive Yanmar tractor to negotiate my paddocks and hills with less difficulty than my old grey Fergy.

As my city work multiplied – at one point there were three part-time jobs – I found that I needed to find residence in the city. It actually suited me quite well, and it seemed I was happiest when splitting my time between city and country. I needed the close human contact of ministry which farm work did not offer, yet the solitude and silence of the farm was an amazing resource. The pattern of my earliest years on the farm, when I was in full-time parish work, was re-established.

Meeting a Filipina at a theological conference in India, I had no inkling how significant the encounter would prove. Nor did I share with Sophia at that stage my passion for farming – as far as she was concerned, I was merely a theologian. Some ten years and after both our marriages failed, we realised that our lives belonged together.

Sophia's first visit to the farm left her nonplussed. 'Where are the neighbours? And where are the workers?' she inquired.

I was able to point out the start of the neighbour's property over the hill, though no actual people appeared! Farming in the Australian environment and economy is far different from the corresponding enterprise in the Philippines! At some point, it must have emerged for her that this was a major component of the life she was joining.

At first, she struggled with my wish and need to spend regular weekends at the farm. But there was always work to be done, stock to be visited. Her first recorded labour on the farm was road mending, as our gravel hillside entry road eroded after winter rains and needed continual repair. During Easter early in our years together, Sophia conceived and organised a retreat for Black Saturday when we set up stations of the cross at various points around the dry farm landscape. It was wonderfully successful, as our farm was within commuting distance of the city, and the insertion of late summer scenes into the familiar Easter ritual stimulated imaginations and spirits. Other retreats followed, including one for new clergy introducing them to a Noongar perspective on the land and spirituality.

Sophia's love of photography emerged and her frequent walks around the farm became the occasion for documenting the changing seasons and the beauties of our bushland vistas. Meanwhile, I refined my farming practice with a good group of Black Angus cows and a compliant little bull, and regularly made good returns at the Muchea cattle saleyards. New dimensions of the farm and its meaning in our lives took shape.

As an ethical farmer, I was never very happy about the use of herbicides in my cropping practice. However, with the invasion of weeds into the carefully seeded oats, I found applications of the glyphosate to be necessary. After several successful crops, an invasion of wild turnip ruined the year's hay harvest. It was the final nail in the coffin of a traditional cropping routine.

At roughly that time, I began to read about regenerative agriculture, in some ways, a new development at the end of the twentieth century, in other ways a revival of time-honoured practices. In the United States, where I pursued graduate studies and then became a lecturer in theology, I discovered the writings of Wendell Berry and was drawn to his non-industrial and traditional methods. But the encounter with Charles Massy's monumental *Call of the Reed Warbler: A New Agriculture, a New Earth* in 2020 set my whole approach to farming on a new course.

It now appears that the developments in Australian agriculture in the years following the Second World War, while producing a great increase in yield, were actually harmful to the fertility of the soil. Aside from the obvious issues of soil erosion and salination, there were deeper problems just beneath the surface. Developed during the chemical stage of agricultural science, our practice relied heavily on the application of herbicides and fertilisers. While the destructive effects of ploughing emerged early in the second half of the century, it was not until the 70s and 80s that the study of the life beneath the soil, at the level of micro-biology, emerged and the discovery that usual methods of farming were in fact destructive of this level of soil function.

A failed crop in 2022 convinced me of the need for a change of practice. The heavily ploughed paddock would be rested and no more superphosphate to be applied, as I concentrated on improving the soil biome. While resting the soil, I sought to encourage the emergence of native grasses, with some planting of such varieties as kangaroo grass and saltbush. Stock could graze the emerging grasslands only intermittently to allow some natural regeneration to occur. Oats would only be seeded when the grassland was well established.

Another section of remnant bushland on a hillside could

be restored if it was protected from grazing stock. A significant fencing project was indicated. Fortunately, some retired farmers from Kalamunda were willing to assist with the project and soon new fences began to appear. A project of conserving remnant bushland now covered part of the property.

Up to that point, I had simply allowed the animals to graze the entire property year-round – with a small acreage, I thought that there would be little benefit in any other arrangement. Reading Massy, however, I became convinced of the benefits of rotational grazing, and so another fencing project was called for. It became the next step in seeking to make regenerative use of the farm.

The more I read, the more excited I became. The new approach was music to my ageing ears. A new start for an old farm and an old farmer! What could be more important at this phase of my life than to be giving back to the good earth in this way? The farm that has rewarded me in so many ways called for a kind of care and management that would restore it to something like its original fertility. My spirit too would thereby be renewed.

Charles Massy speaks of the impact of regenerative agriculture on its practitioners, and it seems that out of the lifelong partnership the purchase of a farm entails, rewards emerge in a kind of mutuality between land and farmer that moves us beyond the utilitarian to the spiritual. I thought of the deep bonds that are present in Indigenous land practices and was thrilled to think of an affinity. I hesitate to call my connection with the farm a symbiosis, for I know at times it is important for me to get away. However, there is a kind of reciprocal relationship has emerged out of what began as a financial transaction. This is where, for me, the physical and the spiritual meet, where poetry and farming embrace one another.

> The rest is poetry…
> Fifty-five acres is my lot in life
> not much by some standards
> but enough by others, bountiful
> and wondrous to ageing eyes.
>
> From 'September Song'

Meditation on Arrival at Farm

Silence like a blanket
wraps you in its folds.

Only a chorus of magpies
pierces the stillness.

Come and stay here
listen for the music.

A gentle rain rustles
rooftop keeps you dry.

Like darkness
restfulness draws you in

quiet, dry, protected.
Rapt in wonder.

The Farm Year

Early Autumn Days

The dog days of summer snap at the toes of autumn
trying to gain a foothold in the old fading year
paddocks and hill are deathly grey with faded grasses
and farmers wait with eager plans for this year's seeding.

Man and beast and the land itself must pause
until the season breaks with wind and rain
and all seem fervourless and glum
as days stay hot and dryness spreads around.

The dregs of summer clog the cup
of autumn and its new year festivals
but the ceremonies of death claim the land
and not one shire is ready to break forth.

So we wait, and in our waiting scan the western skies
for some hint of cloud, of change, of a break
to signal a new season, a new beginning.
Skies are porcelain blue with not a crack in sight.

The Coming of the Rain

We were just sipping Shiraz
watching the colours of sunset
on the western veranda
when distant thunder sounded
and flashes lit the horizon.

By the time darkness fell
a gentle rustling on the roof.
It's come, I cried in exultation,
an answer to prayer. Dry earth
soaked up the first moisture
in months, dust receded and
once again fertile soil received.

Seeds, long buried started
to swell with new life. Even cows,
accustomed to dry feed now
anticipated the return of fresh
green feed, at least in mind's eye.
Oh joy, we cried. Thanks be.

Ploughing

Around and around you go
the diesel's steady pulse
keeps the huge wheels turning
the plough bumps and slices
across the damp earth. What lies beneath
is rich brown loam, opened and lifted
by the ranked series of discs
green shoots roll over into the tilth.

The work is certainly tedious
but you are not bored.
Each line is different,
colours that greet your eyes
smell of freshly broken ground.
Soon the paddock takes on
the fresh look of expectation
awaiting new arrivals.

Around and around you go
in ever diminishing circuits.
There's something ancient, primal
as you turn green pasture
into a tilled field, ready for seeding.
Who could be bored
an endless parade of death
giving over to life rising again?

Lap of Luxury

Old ute cranks, fires first time,
down the grassy slope on a victory lap
dog on my knee, nose thrust
out in the wind, notice dry pasture,
trees showing heat stress, branches dropping
but what are we hoping to find?

Eyes seek out the black cattle
quietly grazing in the hill above the trough
but it is not profit from these
companions, life forms
who inhabit this place peaceably,
bring their natural increase,
thinning of rank growth.

Across the fence, pasture is thick
destocked months back, neighbours
make their own decisions – this year
we're more lightly stocked
for summer drought and feed loss.
Neither of us makes money.

Turning back at the tank gate
retrace tracks uphill and around
to the dam – losing water
to evaporation and seepage –
will hold up a few more weeks,
animals wade deep for a clear drink.

Just an idle lap really
not so much victory as luxury:
for the beauty of all this process –
progress be damned
we keep the place going,
the old ute running.

September Song

Fifty-five acres is my lot in life
not much by some standards
but enough by others, bountiful
and wondrous to ageing eyes.

I see the results of many years
of hard work, first with Dad,
then alone, keeping fences
intact and oat crops yielding

plenty for my small herd
lots for me and for the dog
lying at my feet, glad to be
here this sunny September day.

November Storm

Square bales are in the shed
round bales rest in the paddocks
which is fine for they shed
rainwater just beginning to fall.

Summer's great dying well
under way, patches of brown
spreading all over
only pockets of green remaining.

So what's this
sudden unseasonal rain
too late to build anything
a top up for our tanks?

No matter; poles swing
without regard for climatic events.
We bless our good fortune
a rich harvest secure

good health in herd and soil,
rain in November,
plenty of summer feed,
some of it already home.

After Harvest

Of course, you love the ploughing,
summer feeding of hungry beasts
but the best feeling all year
come rain or shine is crop secure
shed full of baled hay.
You swing the door shut to keep out
inquisitive cattle and stray kangaroos.

This year, a new shed packed
to the rafters with aromatic hay
grown on our few acres of arable land
no matter it's weed infested
eager cattle will munch
in lean dry months ahead.
For a week or so, as days lengthen
and temps soar, you rest
with this thought – harvest home.

Resting Cows

First thing in the day
cows nose furiously
as he rolls out the big bale.

Across the fence a herd
complains loudly, seeing hay
and wires that separate.

The day blows in hot.
By eleven, both groups
take to the shade.

His own herd seem to luxuriate
there, hay strewn around
an afternoon feed ahead.

He watches them shelter
from the midday sun
glad of the abundant harvest.

There's plenty more
where that came from
but it's a long dry ahead.

On Farming

Half Farmer Half Poet

With apologies to John Kinsella, *Jam Tree Gully*

In my wellies and Drizabones
I stumble out of the drizzle
to the sheltering veranda.
Hungry animals chomp on the lines
of dry green feed I articulate
in their presence – absence
of words bothers them not a whit
as I reach for the laptop and
the whole task comes down to this:

What to say to John Kinsella
so smug in his Jam Tree Gully
no-production model of rural
living, with empty red shed
fences all pulled down?
Well, mate, someone has to do it,
if not you then others, don't
pretend you can survive
on poetry alone.

My shed is green and so too my
production-methods, no less poetic
than yours. Let your uni job
keep your hands warm and
soft for penning lines,
mine grow cold and hard
publishing lines of hay
for mouths that feed us all.

Farming with Trees

In the great fire of '04
many trees fell and burned,
pasture was reduced to ash.
Time to start again.

Just then an old farmer advised
cut down all the rest now
before the Greenies take over.
I thought of Reagan's dictum

'Cut down all the trees,
Jesus is coming.'*
Such arrant nonsense
doesn't push good farming.

A sustainable mix of pasture
and trees suits me well.
Still, twenty years after the fire
I marvel at new life,

sharpen my blades
go among the sprouting growth
to thin out weedy and scrubby
that others may grow tall and thrive.

---

* Attributed to James Watt, President Reagan's Secretary of the Interior

Saving the Universe

the safekeeping of the small acreages of the universe…entrusted to
us – Wendell Berry

It's come to this according to my guru
not the little ones, our family members
we have to guard, but the small farms
we keep in back blocks and backyards.

Around them gather subdividers
and agents, agribusiness men
who wish to turn a profit, accumulate
more by monocultures of destruction.

A friend wants to sell me his land
and I sure want to buy it, yet
by some grace of impecunity,
I say, No. What I have is enough.

It passes to another instead
I have now a neighbour to help me
with my work, together we practise
safekeeping of the universe in our trust.

Salt Burn

Row upon row of upright wheat stalks
each bearing its gift of ripening grain
just over the hill and down the slope
starts the salt, now in white and pink
with only salt bush surviving the scald.

Dead tree trunks gesticulate toward the sky
as if to protest the violence done to this
once gentle wooded landscape – for man
must come and clear the trees for crops
and with the felling of the last tree cover,
inexorably salt rises and land is poisoned.

Dead now for a thousand years, a seeping curse
turning our sweeping landscapes into desert.
Salt spreads, land dies before our eyes
more fertiliser is pumped onto the surface
to produce one more crop for this year's harvest,
preparing for the bitter harvest of years
to come. Driving through this country, we marvel
at the ingenuity of man, a fury of destruction.

Morality Play

All over the sunburnt country
on hills, by rivers, on flattened plains
the dirt is turning white;
a silent snow
that falls from below. – Dennis Haskell, *Inland Sea*

Was not the sun
that burnt it white.
The hand of man
felled the tree and hurt
ancient red dirt.

Silent now, in hills
and flattened plains, but then
he claimed his triumph
with whoop and shout
another giant taken out.

Later came a rain of tears
as distant sons sowed
hope on blighted ground –
and lost their bounty
a sorry sunburnt country.

Bruce Rock Dreaming

As a process…the muting of a large part of humanity by European colonisers cannot be separated from the simultaneous muting of 'Nature'. – Amitav Ghosh, *The Nutmeg's Curse*

Mile upon mile of open crop lands,
wheat, canola and barley still green,
beyond human scale. Giant machines
pass over at seed time and harvest…
seldom visited let alone inhabited
depopulated, without song or story
visited only in pursuit of profit.

The generations who once roamed
and danced these places
have been erased, without memorial.
In bustling Bruce Rock we found no
mention of those folk who lived
here so long before – an eerie silence
to cover an ancient theft?

The muting of the land is apparent
in these vast swaths of industrial landscape.
Is Australian agriculture the latest expression
of the colonial enterprise and impulse?
Or are we settlers, yet to learn
the true nature of this place?

More Land

He lays a hand upon my arm
looks me square in the eye
mate, we want to sell our land
we'd like to offer it to you.

I take the old wagon and drive the rutted track
up the Galloway block, longer and deeper
than my neighbouring property.
And then the all-year dam at back!
Such beautiful land, so close
it would be madness to let it slip.

I do my sums – if I sell this and that,
cash in my super then maybe just.
By running twenty steers I could make 2 grand…
It is enough? Almost, a real stretch
with no reserves.

Some folk come to us as friends
but we must drive them off.
Jesus said, Get behind me Satan
to his closest disciple, Peter.

Haltingly I say my Noes,
and the circus begins without me
an agent is hired, signs go up
a chance slips away, my finger itch
take up an old volume of E.F. Schumacher
bloody small is bloody beautiful!

Sufficiency

It is enough
this hillside
my dog to run free
cows grow fat.

I crank up the old ute
a tour of inspection.
Overnight, nothing has moved
cattle munch hay, fires
die down, grass is damp
with early morning dew.

Naturally, I could desire more
but if the Lord is shepherd
leading into green pastures
by still waters
I shall not want.

From the Hilltop

Hymn

That day in '89 sealed my fate
when I bought the farm. The 'block'
she wanted to call it. I said, 'farm'!
Did I glimpse already the spread of today?

It was only a block, boundary-fenced
with a rough and rutted track up the ridge.
a tank and a trough, not much in the way
of work history, super history the salesman lied.

At first it was all work, old Bert and I
built a little shed from garnered iron, salvaged
lumber. Some fences constructed
time to plough with rented tractor.

Our first herd, eight nor-wester steers
brought a modest profit, and a great
encouragement to enterprise.
Soon there were a dozen small steers

It seemed we could make a go of it.
Cattle yards were built with old lumber
and wandoo posts, hard, handwork
by Bert and me over many months,

As funds waxed and waned, new road
steel framed shed, a brick house on the hill.
It seemed we were building a home.
A crop was planted, someone baled it.

We lost Dad in '99, but now Sophia joined
the party, time to plant an orchard.
Tahitian limes were chosen, we
planted and soon a line of irrigation.

One day last year my eyes were opened and
I started to write – at once it became my muse.
Now I have no other and so a hymn of praise
I raise, to this beloved farm and to that day.

After the Fire

Driving west, at last reaching that final
bend in the road, I see posts are
gone and the gate flattened –
ring-lock and barb a tangled mess.

All before me is ashen
pasture, tree trunks black,
fallen where they burned
now blocking the drive.

Car abandoned, I continue on foot.
Fences all down and cattle yards –
so carefully built with old Bert,
just charred shards. Sharp debris

crunches underfoot staining my shoes
black beyond hope. But then I see it
on the far hill – iron roof shimmering.
A benediction in morning sunlight.

The Magic Windmill

A lever is pulled. The yellow tail
swings into line behind the big fan.

Gathering speed, rods push and pull
fresh water out of dry ground.

I watch it swing this way and that
lifting from the depths an old story.

A wooden crate from windswept Chicago
making its way to the dusty railway siding

at Perenjori on the Midland line.
A boy sits wide-eyed as Pop

plays with his giant Meccano set.
And look! The pieces fit together.

Excitedly the old man joins strut to cog
frame to stand, and soon an entire Aermotor

is turning smoothly in the hot dust.
All that remains is to put it up.

Sixty years later, my aged father
dreams of a new Aermotor cranking

on the Chittering farm we work together.
OK Dad, let's do it. You make the calls,

I'll foot the bills. Months pass,
a year, nothing happens. To his dying day

he dreamt of this magic windmill.
Wouldn't it be lovely is all he would say.

I will sit for hours – the yellow tail
spins its potent spell.

A spring rises up – no longer alone
I'm seeing Perenjori through his eyes.

This my real

Less than viable acres,
steel shed, tractor, ancient hay baler.
Windmill pumps slightly saline water
drunk by breeding herd, bull with balls
cows have calves, sell for good price.
What's not to love here? Sophie stays away,
can't manage the hill with gravel.

No Bickley Valley hobby farm
white post and rail tax-dodging fences.
Steel pegs with rusting barb and ring-lock here,
This place my real, house plain enough
to keep off rain, warm in winter
cool in summer, welcome guests
dwell in peace or splendid isolation.

It's dusty, gritty, dirt smudges
every corner. No city spotless,
rainwashed streets, ornamental trees,
but marri, wandoo. Here
I stake my claim as near as
I can get to real farm.

Marginal Farm

What saves it is to love the farming – Wendell Berry, 1980

Rocky slopes, tree lined,
some steep some gentle
fall away to a few acres
of rich loamy soil.

My views are stunning
out across valley bottoms
and peaks. We admire
from a distance.

Husbandry here
with eroded pastures
few acres to till
profits little

Unless the seed
and harvest are one
a saving love
for hillside farming.

Wendell Berry, *The Unsettling of America: Culture and Agriculture.*
(San Francisco: Sierra Club Books, 1977)
The Art of Loading Brush: New Agrarian Writings. (Berkeley,
California: Counterpoint, 2017)

Gold mine

It was a Noongar elder told me
you're sitting on a gold mine
here, confirmed in me the belief
since first I saw these acres.

Within my range, my pocket
set against the hillside
in simple elegance, a track
winding up to its summit.

You mine for gold if greedy
but I resolved to be less than that
run a few sheep, some cattle
make only modest gains.

My Noongar brother meant for me
to cherish my gold mine
not dig it up, nurture the flow
follow its songlines.

As I walk, I enjoy my herd
foraging the feed which grows
in abundance, glad
to squander my gold on them.

Seeking

I return again
to the hillside farm
I am forever leaving.

Week about I come
with any excuse
save the truth.

Feed the cattle
plough up ground
sow a seed.

What is the need
lodged deep within
not found in these?

Fickle man I am
forever seeking
for what gain?

Find a place where love
may grow, return
again to hillside farm

No end there is
arrive to leave again
in search of haven.

Bountiful Acres

My beautiful acres
green in morning sunlight
oats on bottom land
limes in uphill orchard.

Good to grow anything
crop sprouting and cows
fattening on lush pasture.
Such bountiful acres.

In late afternoon
shadows lengthen
cross overgrown pathways.
I sit in quiet repose

Wonder, will it grow
me old, bear me safe
unto the end, boundless
beauteous acreage?

More Like a Sabbath

I'm so thankful
just to be here,
sitting by an open window
a good book at hand
and signs of heavenly gifting
all around. It is not a workday,
more like a sabbath, rest to enjoy
the growth of saltbush
sound of cattle with cut hay
song of kookaburra, magpie.
Here I raise my Ebenezer
hither by thy help I've come.*
Gentle breezes speak of the
source of all benevolence
I have known. Blessed be.

* Robert Robinson, 'Come, Thou Fount of Every Blessing'

www.ingramcontent.com/pod-product-compliance
Lightning Source LLC
Chambersburg PA
CBHW071037080526
44587CB00015B/2660